UNTITLED

BY
THOMAS A. MASSAQUOI

Published by Thomas Massaquoi

Copyright © 2016 Thomas A. Massaquoi

First Printing, 2016

ISBN 978-0-692-82417-7

www.thomasmassaquoi.com

CONTENTS

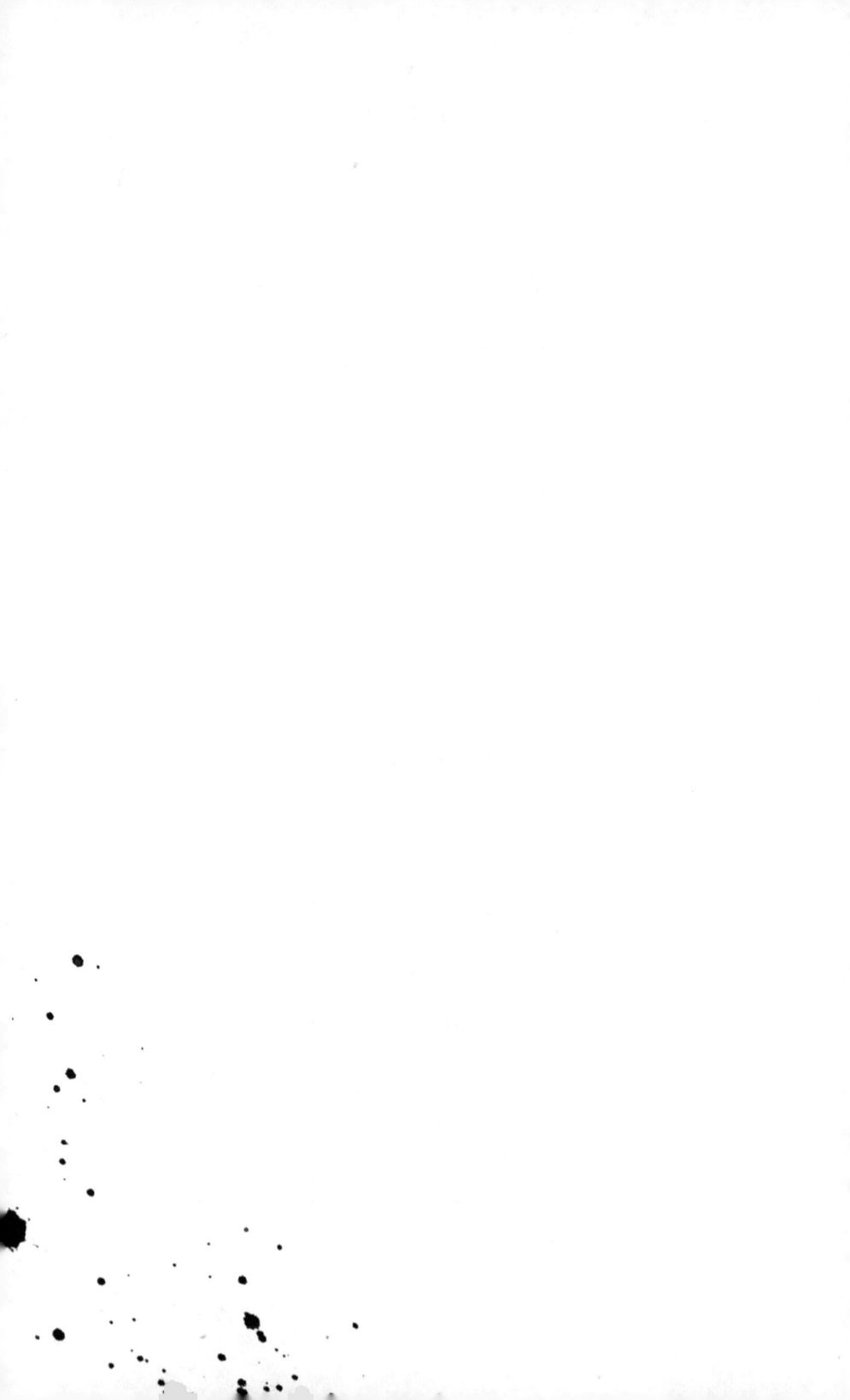

I originally began writing poetry at the age of 8. I took a break and felt inspired to write again. These 33 poems are expressions, feelings and emotions I have felt over the past two years. I hope you enjoy.

Arthur.

UNTITLED I

When I first met you it was,

Simple.

Easy.

Casual.

Those genuine eyes and provocative smile was a strange
yet familiar feeling. You transitioned beyond a stranger.

I found you again professing your thoughts,

I Listened.

I paused.

I believed.

You kissed me slowly and told me you wanted to feel my
heart beat.

My heart pulsed.

My mind cleared.

My thoughts engaged.

In that moment I surrendered to you all that I had
guarded,

Power.

Control.

Fear.

UNTITLED II

I want to sit next to you on a train.

Your coat brushing against mine.

Your head resting on my shoulder as I stare out the
window, watching the world fly by.

Your protector. Your hero. Your guardian.

Your hand against mine. Our fingers locking in unison,
cold rings warmed by our energies.

Existing in your truth. You became my muse.
Tragic, yet beautiful.

I want to discover me more, by discovering you.

UNTITLED III

I do not know what to call this, but I like it.

I don't want to lose that feeling when I see your
name appear.
Our conversation at all levels is treasured
and dear.

How will this manifest?
Something great or less.
An intrinsic high, vibrant in darkness.

If this unburdens or imprisons your soul.
Even if it is not to me. I want to see you run, soar and
break free.

If we both let go and trust in moments like this.
Feelings and challenges like this.

We may move towards absolution and adoration.

I sat at the bench on a cold winter day.
Seasons changed.
Day turned into night and night turned into day.

The life I had built had forsaken me, forsaken us,
forsaken all of this.
Casualties of reality and honesty for the life wanted,
to be shared with the most desired.

Hubris was our anthem in the battle of self-doubt.
When we began, I controlled the warfare in my heart,
but now I find myself steady like a boat on a stream,
rowing, rowing, rowing...

UNTITLED V

I held your hand as we watched the world fall apart.
Broken together, you were always near, yet always far.

As things tumbled and crumbled I remained.
Even through fire and storms, silence was sustained.

I sat with you. I sat with you.

Like elements in nature, we discovered our emotions.
Lovely, powerful, the divine.

We did more than simply survive.

As we grew together, we thrived...

As we grew together, we watched the world fall apart...

UNTITLED VI

I understood long ago that our
decisions would come to this.
That we would do more than learning
to live, love and forgive.

The burdens we strayed from, elevate and discovered,
make us similar, conscious, vulnerable.

How do we survive, how did we survive?

We sought refuge amongst each other when
the water had risen and oxygen ran out.

Love manifests when we found ourselves.
Believed in ourselves.

By seeking exclusively the present.
We negated the past and denied the future.
We found progress.

UNTITLED VII

The autumn rain fell on our faces.
As we stood there in silence, waiting.
Waiting for the other to say goodbye.

As water drenched your shirt, jeans and shoes.
I looked in your eyes.
I couldn't look past you.

We've gotten all we wanted from here.

How could I ask for more?
How could I ask more of this?

I want to see your face on the other side of the sun.
I want to sit and talk with you in a quiet room.
I want to slow dance with you to the static of a radio.

I want to cuddle with you and get sick as a result of
the same thing.
I want to get naked and swim in the ocean with you.
I want to smell the flowers of the New England spring
when brushed against you.

I want to laugh with you, even when all I want to do
is cry.

UNTITLED IX

From the moment I saw you, I knew I wanted to know
everything about you.

The passion and desire in your heart caught my attention.
I extended. You reciprocated.

When I opened the door I saw you standing there tall, tan,
emerald eyes. The first words you spoke put me at ease.
You were quiet, but confident and settled.

If I couldn't have you, I wanted to be your friend.

Even if it was from a far.

My spirit was content with this fact and truth.

In my mind and heart, I would have lit this world on fire
if you asked me too.
Not sure if it's infatuation, lust, passion, love or
friendship. Whatever it is.
I respect you and everything you stand for.

It's that same respect that locked me away from you.

The same that has me now a spectator of your life rather
than a participant.

The same that has me wishing there could have been more
time.

UNTITLED X

Aren't you tired of fighting?
Yelling. Screaming. Raging.

Picking apart your brother.
Raping your sister.
Denying your mother.
Cursing your father.

Everything you are seeking you already have, but
your thirst and want for more has not been filled.

It will not be filled.

I will continue believing in you until you are able
to believe in yourself.

I will hold onto hope until you are ready to hold
onto it yourself.

UNTITLED XI

Why can't we be friends.

Why can't we sit for a while.

Why can't we converse for a while.

You keep pushing me away as if I've passed away.

Why won't you see me like you see them.

Why won't you acknowledge me like you acknowledge them.

Why won't you hear me like you hear them.

I am still here.

I am still alive.

I am still breathing.

UNTITLED XII

I swore to God I wouldn't forgive you.

I swore to myself I would re-write this story.

I promised myself I would do better than her.

Everything she denied herself I would not do the same
yet here I am.

Toxic.

I wish I was a praying man, but I cannot find resolve.

I cannot find resolution.

I cannot find peace.

So I'll just sleep. All I can do, is sleep.

UNTITLED XIII

You and I were never meant to fly so close to the sun.

God gave us wings but did not want to forsake us.

We had gravity.

Gravity.

Denied.

Lied to.

Pissed away.

Waiting patiently for you to say my name.

You asked.

I answered.

You pushed away.

I will wait to hear from you.

I will wait for you to say my name.

UNTITLED XV

I'm locked outside.

Tortured and wondering why...

Why was time, nor you, never on our side.

I was wanting to know you.

I was wanting to lay and sit next to you.

I wanted to cry with you.

If it was close or from afar.

My life was already complete but I wanted you.

The articulate soldier.

UNTITLED XVI

Broken men raise broken children.

Children are a reflection of adults.

Aspiring to keep up with what they witnessed.

The advanced.

The refined.

The good.

The bad.

The damned.

Forever was just a word, as I listened to Prince on
the radio.

Like doves cry and try to fly.

I denied myself the truth.

It had become immutable that things couldn't stay the same.

As I fought for this, you watched it burn.

I was your casualty.

I was your collateral damage.

I was you and you were me.

I loved your tattoos.

I loved your hair.

I loved your eyes.

I loved your voice.

I loved our drives.

I loved your laugh.

I loved your tears.

I loved your faults.

I loved your body.

I loved your brokenness.

I loved your madness.

I loved the way you lied.

UNTITLED XIX

I drove in the darkness to reach you.

When I got to the door I could see you with him.

It was silent. It was quiet.

I was no longer a part of your story.

My chapter was over.

I turned around. I walked to the car.

I got in. I didn't start the car.

I sat there.

UNTITLED XX

I wanted to say something prolific.

I wanted to say something iconic.

I wanted to show you something different.

I wanted to show you something tasteful.

I can't take my eyes off you.

For I have every right to speak my pain.

Speak my truth.

As I walk on this crystal beach, feeling the cold water crash against my feet, all I can do is keep focus on you.

Focus.

Pulsating lights.

City lights.

Fade to black.

Good people. City people. Paper people.

Hollow. Mellow. Shallow. Yellow.

Envy.

Transcendent. Immaculate.

Intrinsic.

Sex is more than physical.

It's positive versus negative.

Electric. Tantric. Iconic.

It was never a game we could win.

Why deny ourselves the deep pleasures of the spirit.

As we found love in this hopeless place.

We also found spiritual pleasure.

Electric. Tantric. Iconic.

More than the physical.

I held the key in my hand as you walked out the door.

You looked away as I begged you to stay.
Your hand holding the door.

I whispered I loved you, but I couldn't bring myself
to yell it or profess it.

I knew you needed to go, so I didn't fight fate or my
truth.

Yes, you needed to leave.

Without any hesitation.

If it's anything you need.

It can no longer be grown here.

I found resolution and peace in the ending of this, in
closing the door and holding this key.

The Texas streets are wild and beautiful.

The people eclectic and prolific.

Diverse.

The sky blue and grey in the same moments.

The tea as fresh as the spring waters boiled in.

Yes.

Diverse.

These Texas streets are wild and beautiful.

In Blue.

In Grey.

If we never got together I would not be sitting
here thinking.

If we never got together I would not be reflecting.

If we never got together I would not be crying.

If we never got together I would never have
found myself.

If we never got together I would never have found
my own strength.

If we never got together I would never become my
own champion.

So I guess I owe you now.

Isn't this ironic.

UNTITLED XXVII

I want you to know there is hope.

Hope is in you and me.

In the universe.

The water, oceans and streams.

It's simple. Just look in the water...

What do you see?

Sweet, sweet child of mine.

The devil isn't in you.

They lie.

They lie.

They lie.

They see in you the very thing that can destroy them.
What they could not manifest within them.

Love.

They lie.

They lie.

They lie.

I came across a dime.

I placed it in my pocket.

I took it home.

I put in my mason jar.

There it sat.

As I grew.

It remained.

Years turned into decades.

It still remained.

It was a constant of who I was and yet to become.

I want passion.

Fire.

Heat.

Desire.

I am not seeking lust or the temporary.

I want to feel power.

Seduction.

Sensuality.

Intimacy.

I want unrestrained, raw and uninhibited energy.

Come to me.

I felt the resistance.

I saw the fight.

The blood stained on the floor.

The sounds of chaos and madness are deafening.

The rage and ignorance blinding.

The depression and defeat.

Saddening.

Peace we've longed for is fading.

Diminishing.

Can you spare some time.

Talk with me a while.

I was the fool. I lied.

I thought I knew more.

Understood it all.

As I age I recognize I was never the center.

I was one of many.

Never content and my spirit unsteady.

Progress has always been within my reach.

I've scraped and crawled.

Now looking to it with bended knees.

In glory of knowing this is the end my time.

It has now expired.

Well done life. Well done.

UNTITLED XXXIII

Rhythm in black.

Rhythm in peace.

Rhythm in silence.

Rhythm in motion.

Rhythm in knowing.

Rhythm in feeling.

Rhythm in dying.

A WORD FROM THE AUTHOR

Educate. Inspire. Grow.

ABOUT THE AUTHOR

A Philosopher with a camera, pen and paper. I have spent my life traveling the world, learning about culture and social development. A graduate of Philosophy from The University of Texas at Arlington, I have used my experiences to help others in advocacy for a better world. I'm a Writer, Activist, Philanthropist, Mediator, Humanitarian and Philosopher. An active participant in the global community, visual art and writing is a medium I use for creative and artistic expression. I'm currently based in Texas.

www.ingramcontent.com/pod-product-compliance
Lightning Source LLC
Chambersburg PA
CBHW060951050426
42337CB00054B/4428